How Do I Say That?

¿Cómo se dice...?

by/de Sue Wise
Illustrated by/Illustraciones de Christine Coirault

GARETH**STEVENS**
GS
PUBLISHING
A Member of the WRC Media Family of Companies

Please visit our web site at: www.garethstevens.com
For a free color catalog describing Gareth Stevens Publishing's
list of high-quality books and multimedia programs, call
1-800-542-2595 (USA) or 1-800-387-3178 (Canada).
Gareth Stevens Publishing's fax: (414) 332-3567.

Library of Congress Cataloging-in-Publication Data available upon request from
publisher. Fax (414) 336-0157 for the attention of the Publishing Records Department.

ISBN 0-8368-6259-7 (lib. bdg.)
ISBN 0-8368-6583-9 (softcover)

This edition first published in 2006 by
Gareth Stevens Publishing
A Member of the WRC Media Family of Companies
330 West Olive Street, Suite 100
Milwaukee, Wisconsin 53212 USA

This U.S. edition copyright © 2006 by Gareth Stevens, Inc. Original
edition copyright © 2005 by Bookwork, Ltd. First published in 2005
by Pangolin Books.

ELL Editorial Staff
Julio Abreu, Editorial Director
Zaida A. Cintron, Editor
Carolyn A. Schildgen, Associate Editor
Phillip Gill, Graphic Designer

Gareth Stevens editor: Dorothy L. Gibbs
Gareth Stevens design: Scott M. Krall
Gareth Stevens production: Jessica Morris

Printed in the United States of America

1 2 3 4 5 6 7 8 9 10 09 08 07 06

Contents
(Contenido)

MENSAJE ESPECIAL SOBRE LA PRONUNCIACIÓN
La guía para la pronunciación de palabras en inglés es una aproximación. En algunos casos, los sonidos en inglés no tienen un sonido equivalente en español, como: la **th**- en **the**, la **j** en **juice**, y ciertas vocales. (Para la **j** en inglés se ha usado la combinación de **dy**.) Por consiguiente, se le recomienda al estudiante que repase estos sonidos únicos con un angloparlante que le pueda ayudar a perfeccionar estos sonidos.

Mary, Mark, and Duke
Eat Breakfast in the Kitchen.

[meri, mark, and duk it brekfast in tha kitchen]

Mary, Mark, y Duke desayunan en la cocina.

dish
[dish]
el plato

cupboard
[kabord]
el gabinete

refrigerator ❄
[refridyereitor]
la nevera

eggs
[egs]
los huevos

bowl
[boul]
el tazón

necktie
[nektai]
la corbata

dog leash
[dag lish]
la correa
del perro

milk
[milk]
la leche

I am so hungry!
[ai am so jangri]
¡Tengo tanta hambre!

butter
[bater]
la mantequilla

cereal
[sirial]
el cereal

4

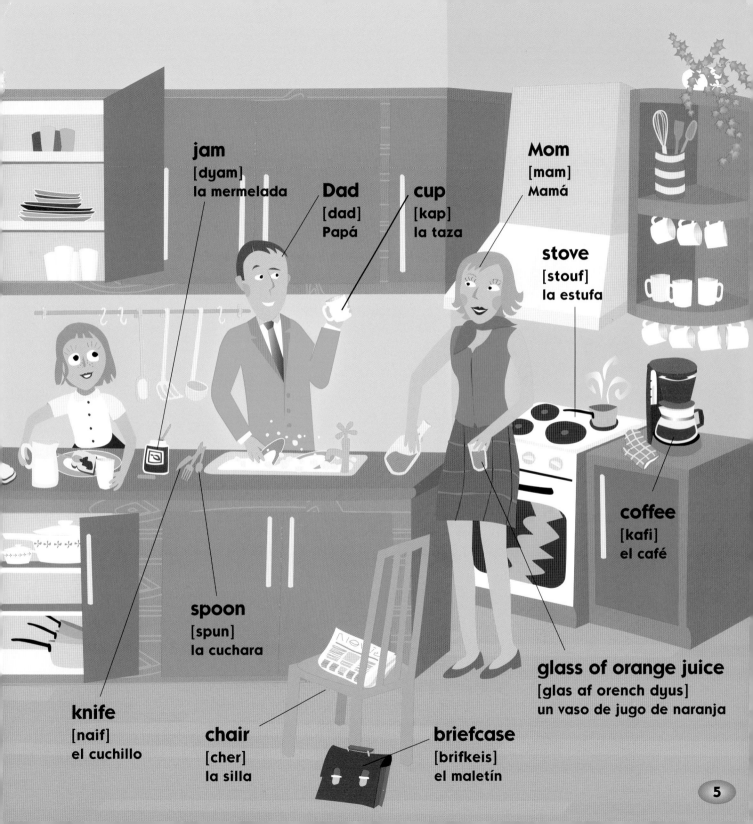

jam
[dyam]
la mermelada

Dad
[dad]
Papá

cup
[kap]
la taza

Mom
[mam]
Mamá

stove
[stouf]
la estufa

coffee
[kafi]
el café

spoon
[spun]
la cuchara

glass of orange juice
[glas af orench dyus]
un vaso de jugo de naranja

knife
[naif]
el cuchillo

chair
[cher]
la silla

briefcase
[brifkeis]
el maletín

5

Can you clean my **knife**, Dad?
I dropped it on the floor.
[kan iu klin mai naif dad? ai drapt it an tha flor]
¿Puedes limpiar mi cuchillo, Papá? Se me cayó al suelo.

Turn off the **stove**! The food is burning.
[tern af tha stouf! tha fud is berning]
¡Apaga la estufa! La comida se está quemando.

Bread tastes much better with some **butter** on it.
[bred teists mach beter uith sam bater an it]
El pan sabe mucho mejor con mantequilla.

Dad loves strawberry **jam**.
[dad lafs straberi dyam]
A Papá le encanta la mermelada de fresa.

I left my school books on the **chair**.
Don't sit on them!
[ai left mai skul buks an tha cher. dont sit an them]
Dejé mis libros de la escuela sobre la silla. ¡No te sientes en ellos!

Mom says that **milk** is good for your bones.
[mam ses that milk is gud for iur bons]
Mamá dice que la leche es muy buena para los huesos.

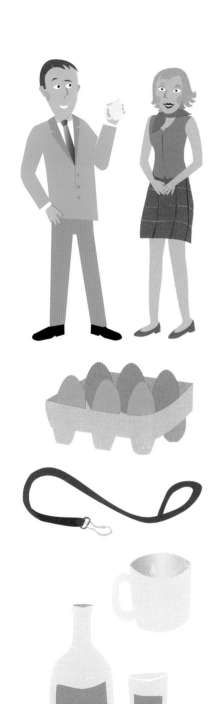

My **mom** is very nice. She makes my breakfast every morning.

[mai mam is veri nais. shi meiks mai brekfast evri morning]
Mi mamá es muy amable. Me hace el desayuno todas las mañanas.

Dad is never late for work.

[dad is nefer leit for uerk]
Papá nunca llega tarde al trabajo.

I like **eggs** for breakfast.

[ai laik egs for brekfast]
Para el desayuno me gustan los huevos.

Where's the **dog's leash**?
It's time for Duke's walk.

[uers tha dags lish? its taim for duks uok]
¿Dónde está la correa del perro? Es hora de su paseo.

Mom drinks two **cups** of coffee before she goes to work.

[mam drinks tu kaps af kafi bifor shi gos tu uerk]
Mamá bebe dos tazas de café antes de irse al trabajo.

Every morning I drink a **glass of orange juice**.

[evri morning ai drink a glas af orench dyus]
Bebo un vaso de jugo de naranja todas las mañanas.

The Students Are Busy in Class.

[tha students ar bisi in klas]

Los estudiantes están ocupados en el aula.

gold star
[gol star]
la estrella dorada

number
[namber]
el número

123456789 $2+4=6$
$7-3=$
$abcdefghijk$

globe
[glob]
el globo terráqueo

ruler
[ruler]
la regla

pen
[pen]
el bolígrafo

computer
[kompiuter]
la computadora

mouse
[maus]
el ratón

keyboard
[kibord]
el teclado

teacher
[ticher]
la maestra

If you look out the **window**, the teacher will get angry.
[if iu luk aut tha uindo, tha ticher uil guet angri]
Si miras por la ventana, la maestra se enojará.

I can't draw straight lines without a **ruler**.
[ai kant dra streit lains uithaut a ruler]
No puedo hacer una raya derecha sin una regla.

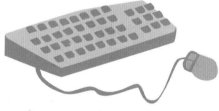

Where are the **pens**? I need to practice writing.
[uer ar tha pens? ai nid tu praktis raiting]
¿Dónde están los bolígrafos? Necesito practicar mi escritura.

I can type on the **Keyboard** without looking.
[ai kan taip an tha kibord uithaut lukin]
Puedo escribir en el teclado sin mirar.

The **fish** lives in a fish bowl.
[tha fish lifs in a fish boul]
El pez vive en la pecera.

Can you lend me a **red** pencil?
[kan iu lend mi a red pensil]
¿Me puedes prestar un lápiz rojo?

I have done a very good **drawing** of a fish.
[ai jaf dan a veri gud drouing af a fish]
He hecho un buen dibujo de un pez.

Look at the **clock** to see what time it is.
[luk at tha klak tu si uat taim it is]
Mira el reloj para saber la hora.

Look for Peru on the **globe**.
[luk for peru an tha glob]
Busca Perú en el globo terráqueo.

Can you close the **door**? It's cold!
[kan iu klos tha dor? its kold]
¿Puedes cerrar la puerta? ¡Hace frío!

My **teacher** tells me that my notebook is not very neat.
[mai ticher tels mi that mai notbuk is nat veri nit]
Mi maestra me dice que mi libreta no está muy ordenada.

Everyone likes to get a **gold star**.
[evriuan laiks tu guet a gol star]
A todo el mundo le gusta recibir una estrella dorada.

The Children and Duke Go to the Supermarket with Mom.

[tha children an duk go tu tha supermarket uith mam]

Los niños y Duke van al supermercado con Mamá.

banana
[banana]
el plátano

cookies
[kukis]
las galletas

cupcake
[kapkeik]
el pastelito

lollipop
[lalipap]
la paleta

beans
[bins]
los frijoles

cheese
[chis]
el queso

Prices are very low.
[praises ar feri lo]
Los precios están muy bajos.

carrot
[kerot]
la zanahoria

tomato
[tomeito]
el tomate

magazine
[magasin]
la revista

newspaper
[nuspeiper]
el periódico

liquid soap
[likuid sop]
el jabón líquido

special offer
[speshal afer]
la oferta especial

dog food
[dag fud]
la comida de perro

bicycle
[baisikel]
la bicicleta

money
[mani]
el dinero

ham
[jam]
el jamón

shopping cart
[shaping kart]
el carrito

cash register
[cash redyister]
la caja

Lollipops are not good for your teeth.
[lalipaps ar nat gud for iur tith]
Las paletas no son buenas para los dientes.

Will you buy this **magazine** for me?
[uil iu bai this magasin for mi]
¿Me compras esta revista?

The **wheel** of the shopping cart sounds like a mouse.
[tha uil af tha shaping kart saunds laik a maus]
La rueda del carrito suena como un ratón.

There are **special offer** signs all over the supermarket.
[ther ar speshal afer sains ol ofer tha supermarket]
Hay ofertas especiales por todo el supermercado.

Don't let the dog steal the **ham**!
[don let tha dag stil tha jam]
¡No dejes que el perro se robe el jamón!

Don't forget the **dog food**.
[dont forguet tha dag fud]
No se te olvide la comida de perro.

I hope it doesn't rain! I left my **bicycle** outside.
[ai hop it dasant rein! ai left mai baisikel autsaid]
¡Espero que no llueva! Dejé mi bicicleta afuera.

Mom says we can't buy any **cookies**.
[mam ses ui kant bai eni kukis]
Mamá dice que no podemos comprar galletas.

Mom took some **cupcakes** to work on her birthday.
[mam tuk sam kapkeiks tu uierk an jer birthdei]
Mamá llevó al trabajo unos pastelitos el día de su cumpleaños.

I spent all my **money** on sweets.
[ai spent ol mai mani an suits]
Me he gastado todo el dinero en dulces.

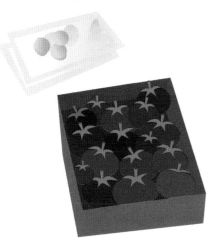

We don't need any **tomatoes**.
[ui dont nid eni tomeitos]
No necesitamos tomates.

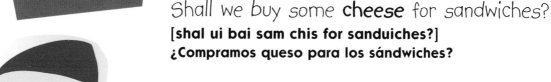

Shall we buy some **cheese** for sandwiches?
[shal ui bai sam chis for sanduiches?]
¿Compramos queso para los sándwiches?

The Children Take Duke
to the Park for a Picnic.

**[tha children teik duk
tu tha park for a picnic]**

**Los niños llevan a Duke
a un picnic en el parque.**

swing
[suing]
el columpio

slide
[slaid]
la resbaladilla
(o la chorrera)

seesaw
[sisa]
el subibaja

pond
[pand]
el estanque

helmet
[jelmet]
el casco

lemonade
[lemaneid]
la limonada

apple
[apel]
la manzana

potato chips
[poteito chips]
las papas fritas

skateboard
[skeitbord]
la patineta

bread
[bred]
el pan

mud
[mad]
el lodo

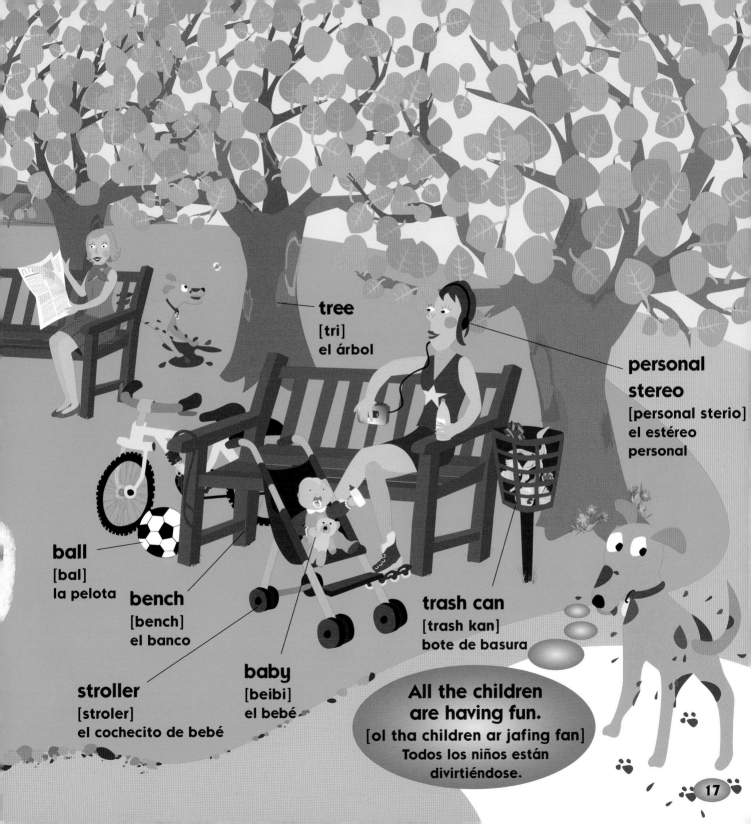

tree
[tri]
el árbol

personal
stereo
[personal sterio]
el estéreo
personal

ball
[bal]
la pelota

bench
[bench]
el banco

trash can
[trash kan]
bote de basura

stroller
[stroler]
el cochecito de bebé

baby
[beibi]
el bebé

All the children
are having fun.
[ol tha children ar jafing fan]
Todos los niños están
divirtiéndose.

17

The **trees** are great for playing hide-and-seek.

[tha tris ar greit for pleing jaidansik]

Los árboles son estupendos para jugar al escondite.

We have lots of fun on the **swings**.

[ui jaf lats af fan an tha suings]

Lo pasamos muy bien en los columpios.

I'm hungry. Can I have some **bread** and cheese?

[aim jangri. kan ai jaf sam bred an chis?]

Tengo hambre. ¿Puedo comer pan con queso?

Mom is sitting on the **bench**.

[mam is sitin an tha bench]

Mamá está sentada en el banco.

Mmm, the **apples** are delicious,
all sweet and juicy.

[mmm, thi apels ar dilishas, ol suit an dyusi]

Mmm, las manzanas están ricas, dulces y jugosas.

I like playing **soccer**, especially when
I score a goal.

[ai laik pleing saker, espeshali uen ai skor a gol]

Me gusta jugar fútbol, especialmente cuando meto un gol.

What are we drinking at the picnic?
Lemonade, of course.
[uat ar ui drinking at tha picnic? lemaneid, af kors]
¿Qué bebemos en el picnic? Limonada, por supuesto.

It hurts when I fall off the **skateboard**.
[it jerts uen ai fal af tha skeitbord]
Me duele cuando me caigo de la patineta.

Be careful! There are lots of wasps by
the **trash can**.
[bi kerful! ther ar lats af uasps bai tha trash kan]
¡Cuidado! Hay muchas avispas alrededor del bote de basura.

My dog likes to play in the **mud**.
[mai dag laiks tu plei in tha mad]
A mi perro le gusta jugar en el lodo.

Will you play on the **seesaw** with me?
[uil iu plei an tha sisa uith mi?]
¿Juegas conmigo en el subibaja?

What fun to eat **potato chips** while playing!
[uat fan tu it poteito chips uail pleing]
¡Qué rico comer papas fritas mientras jugamos!

The Children Wash Duke in the Bathtub.

[tha children uash duk in tha bathtab]

Los niños bañan a Duke en la bañera.

faucet
[facet]
el grifo

toothbrush
[tuthbrash]
el cepillo de dientes

towel
[tauel]
la toalla

I prefer to wash only my face like cats do.
[ai prifer tu uash onli mai feis laik cats du]
Prefiero lavarme sólo la cara como los gatos.

toy boat
[toi bot]
el barco de juguete

sink
[sink]
el lavamanos

underpants
[anderpants]
los calzoncillos

dog collar
[dag caler]
el collar de perro

20

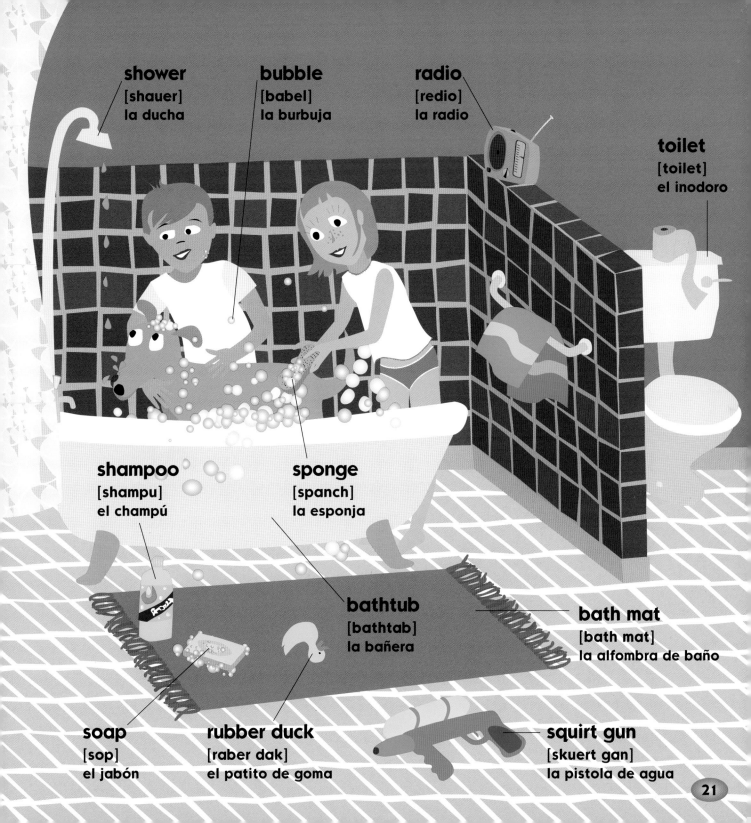

shower
[shauer]
la ducha

bubble
[babel]
la burbuja

radio
[redio]
la radio

toilet
[toilet]
el inodoro

shampoo
[shampu]
el champú

sponge
[spanch]
la esponja

bathtub
[bathtab]
la bañera

bath mat
[bath mat]
la alfombra de baño

soap
[sop]
el jabón

rubber duck
[raber dak]
el patito de goma

squirt gun
[skuert gan]
la pistola de agua

21

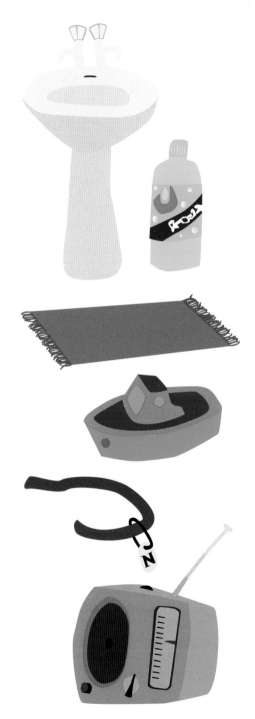

Mom told me to wash my hands in the **sink**.
[mam told mi tu uash mai jands in tha sink]
Mamá me pidió que me lavara las manos en el lavamanos.

The bottle of **shampoo** is nearly empty.
[tha batel af shampu is nirli empti]
La botella de champú está casi vacía.

The **bath mat** is all wet. Who's been splashing?
[tha bath mat is ol uet. jus bin splashing?]
La alfombra de baño está muy mojada. ¿Quién estuvo salpicándola?

When we were little, we used to play
with **toy boats**.
[uen ui uer litel, ui ius tu plei uith toi bots]
Cuando éramos pequeños, jugábamos con barcos de juguete.

The dog likes it when we take off his **collar**.
[tha dag laiks it uen ui teik af jis caler]
Al perro le gusta que le quitemos el collar.

Listen! Your favorite song is on the **radio**.
[lisen! iur feivorit sang is an tha redio]
¡Escucha! Tu canción favorita está en la radio.

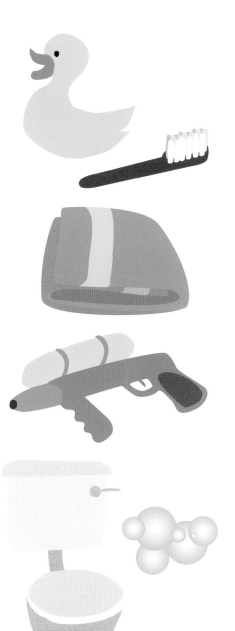

Don't let the dog play with the **toy duck**!
[don let tha dag plei uith tha toi dak]
¡No dejes al perro jugar con el patito de goma!

I lost my **toothbrush**.
[ai last mai tuthbrash]
Perdí mi cepillo de dientes.

It feels good to dry off with a soft **towel**.
[it fils gud tu drai af uith a saf tauel]
Da gusto secarse con una toalla suave.

Dad scolded us when we made a mess
with the **squirt gun**.
[dad skolded as uen ui meid a mes uith tha skuert gan]
Papá nos regañó por mojar el cuarto de baño con la pistola de agua.

I like lots of **bubbles** in the bathtub.
[ai laik lats af babels in tha bathtab]
Me gusta la bañera llena de burbujas.

Hurry up! Dad needs to use the **bathroom**.
[jeri ap! dad nids tu ius tha bathrum]
¡Apúrate! Papá necesita entrar al baño.

It's Time to Go to Bed.
The Children Are Tired.

**[its taim tu go tu bed.
tha children ar taird]**

**Es hora de acostarse.
Los niños están cansados.**

rocket
[raket]
el cohete

poster
[poster]
el cartel

baseball cap
[beisbal kap]
la gorra de béisbol

comic book
[camik buk]
el cómic

**Good night!
Sleep well.**
[gud nait! slip uel]
¡Buenas noches! Que
duermas bien.

sneakers
[snikers]
los zapatos
deportivos

socks
[saks]
los calcetines

pajamas
[padyamas]
la pijama

24

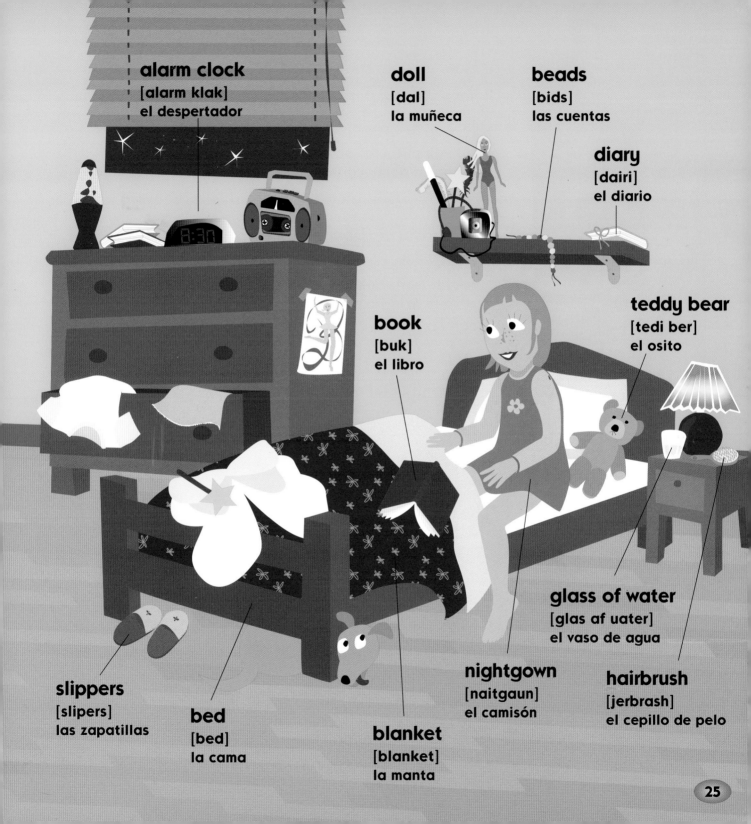

alarm clock
[alarm klak]
el despertador

doll
[dal]
la muñeca

beads
[bids]
las cuentas

diary
[dairi]
el diario

book
[buk]
el libro

teddy bear
[tedi ber]
el osito

glass of water
[glas af uater]
el vaso de agua

slippers
[slipers]
las zapatillas

bed
[bed]
la cama

blanket
[blanket]
la manta

nightgown
[naitgaun]
el camisón

hairbrush
[jerbrash]
el cepillo de pelo

I like putting up **posters** of pop stars in my bedroom.
[ai laik putin ap posters af pap stars in mai bedrum]
Me gusta poner carteles de cantantes en mi dormitorio.

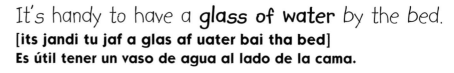

My favorite **book** is so funny that it makes me laugh.
[mai feivorit buk is so fani that it meiks mi laf]
Mi libro favorito es tan divertido que me hace reír.

It's handy to have a **glass of water** by the bed.
[its jandi tu jaf a glas af uater bai tha bed]
Es útil tener un vaso de agua al lado de la cama.

I'd wear my **sneakers** all the time if I could.
[aid uer mai snikers ol tha taim if ai kud]
Yo llevaría puestos mis zapatos deportivos todo el tiempo si pudiera.

Every night, I go to sleep hugging my **teddy bear**.
[evrinait ai gou tu slip jaguing mai tedi ber]
Cada noche me duermo abrazando a mi osito.

You can write your secrets in a **diary**.
[iu kan rait iur sicrets in a dairi]
Puedes escribir tus secretos en un diario.

These **socks** smell really bad!
[this saks smel rili bad]
¡Estos calcetines huelen muy mal!

My **cat** likes to sleep on my bed.
[mai kat laiks tu slip an mai bed]
A mi gato le gusta dormir en mi cama.

I must set the **alarm clock**.
I have to go to school tomorrow.
[ai mast set thi alarm klak. ai jaf tu go tu skul tumaro]
Tengo que poner el despertador. Mañana hay clases.

We often read **comic books** before
going to sleep.
[ui afen rid camik buks bifor gouing tu slip]
A menudo leemos comics antes de dormirnos.

Have you seen my **hairbrush**?
My hair is very tangled.
[jaf iu sin mai jerbrash? mai jer is feri tangeld]
¿Has visto mi cepillo de pelo? Tengo el pelo muy enredado.

My **slippers** keep my feet warm.
[mai slipers kip mai fit uarm]
Mis zapatillas me mantienen calientes los pies.

Practice Your English./Practique el inglés.

Brunch at the Milk and Honey[1] Café

Mary, Mark, and their parents are at The Milk and Honey Café, a restaurant that serves **brunch[2]** *on Sundays.*

Mark: I like brunches because you can eat a lot of different food.

Mary: But you have to be careful, because you can eat too much.

Mark: The last time we went to a brunch, I ate eggs and bacon, pancakes and bagels, toast, apple juice and a piece of cake. Then, I got a **stomach ache[3]**.

Mary: Yes, mine hurt too the last time. I think I ate too much.

Mark: Today I won't make the same mistake. I don't want to feel that way again.

Mary: Me too. I am going to be careful. I am only going to eat **oatmeal[4]**, scrambled eggs, some fruit, and orange juice.

Mark: I am eating pancakes, boiled eggs, apple juice and toast with jam, and maybe cereal.

Mary: Mom says we are eating too much.

Mark: She always says that!

Mark: Oh, oh, I think I did it again! I don't feel too well.

Mary: Yea, Mom was right! We ate too much again.

Mark: It's too bad. We love these brunches—but our stomachs don't!

[1] **honey** [jani]: *miel*
[2] **brunch** [branch]: *desayuno servido al estilo bufé*
[3] **stomach ache** [stamak eik]: *dolor del estómago*
[4] **oatmeal** [otmil]: *avena*

The Missing Pen

Miguel is going to a new school this year. He wants to do well, so he pays attention to everything that **Mrs.[1]** Johnson says. He makes sure he does not spend time looking at the clock or out the window. Each morning, he puts everything he will need in his backpack—his pencil, his pen, his notebook.

Today Miguel is a little **anxious[2]** because Mrs. Johnson will be giving a test in class. The students will write answers to questions she will ask. Miguel studied hard and is sure he will do well. Before the test, students have free time. Some are looking out the window. Some are working at the computer. Some are making drawings. Miguel looks at his notebook one last time. Now, Mrs. Johnson is calling everyone to sit down at their desks for the test. Miguel is ready. He puts a piece of paper in front of him. He reaches for his pen.

And…it isn't there! Did the pen fall out of his backpack? Mrs. Johnson asks the first question. Students start to write their answers. Miguel is now **upset[3]**. He feels like running through the door and hiding in the coatroom. Suddenly, he sees a hand reaching toward him. It is David, one of his new classmates. He smiles and says, "Here, I have an extra pen." Miguel smiles and quickly writes the answer to the first question. He feels relieved. Now, he will **ace the test[4]**! Maybe he has made a friend, too.

[1] **Mrs.** [mises]: *Señora (mujer casada)*
[2] **anxious** [angshas]: *ansioso*
[3] **upset** [apset]: *turbado*
[4] **ace the test** [eis tha test]: *sacar muy buena nota en el examen*

Supermarket Surprise

Mark hates going to the supermarket. His mother brings him there with her because she doesn't want him to stay home alone. But the supermarket is **boring**[1] and he has nothing to do there. When he tries to help his mother with the shopping, she doesn't like it. He tries to remind her to buy things he considers to be important—**ice cream**[2], chocolate, popcorn, and cookies. But his mom thinks other things are more important. She buys potatoes, cheese, apples, lettuce, detergent, deodorant, and toothpaste. Today Mark is especially bored, so he goes to the magazine section. When he gets there, he sees Jessica. She is **one of the nicest**[3] girls in his class. Jessica says hello to him. Suddenly, the supermarket doesn't seem like such a boring place. As Jessica and Mark look at some of the magazines, they talk about school and things that interest both of them. After about 10 minutes, Mark's mom comes down the **aisle**[4] and tells him they are ready to leave. Mark says goodbye to Jessica. Back in the car, Mark's mother is quite surprised to hear Mark say that he would really, really like to come back to the supermarket with her next week.

[1] **boring** [boring]: *aburrido*
[2] **ice cream** [ais crim]: *helado*
[3] **one of the nicest** [naisest]: *una de las más simpáticas*
[4] **aisle** [ail]: *pasillo*

Trouble[1] at Washington Park

It's a beautiful day. The sun is shining and the sky is clear. It is warm and the birds are singing. Washington Park is full of children using the swings and seesaw, riding bicycles on trails, and playing soccer and softball. Some people are sailing on the lake. Many families are having picnics. They are barbecuing hot dogs and hamburgers. The children are also eating fresh fruit and drinking lemonade. Everybody is enjoying a **relaxing**[2] day. But suddenly, a woman starts screaming. Everyone looks in her direction and sees a boy on a skateboard that is going too fast. The boy cannot control his skateboard, and it is **heading straight for**[3] the lake! His mother and his father are both now screaming and running to try to reach him. Then a man who is jogging with his dog sees what is happening. He runs toward the boy. He reaches and grabs the boy just as the skateboard is coming to the edge of the lake! The boy is very scared, but he is not hurt. His parents are very happy, and they thank the jogger over and over again for saving him. People shake the jogger's hand and say he is a hero. Meanwhile, **his dog licks**[4] the boy's face and makes him laugh.

[1] **Trouble** [trabel]: *problema*
[2] **relaxing** [relaksing] *tranquilo y agradable*
[3] **heading straight for** [jeding streit for] *va rumbo directo a*
[4] **his dog licks** [jis dag liks]: *su perro le lame*

Bathroom **Battle**[1]

Mary: Mom, Mark won't come out of the bathroom! Mark, hurry up!

Mark: You should get up earlier.

Mary: Mark, you have been in the bathroom for an hour!

Mark: Leave me alone so that I can finish **brushing my teeth**[2].

Mom: Children, stop screaming and get ready for school.

Mary: I can't get ready, Mom. Mark won't let me use the bathroom. When I get into the bathroom, I have to take a shower and dry my hair.

Mark: All right, all right. I am almost done.

Mary: Mom, he still won't come out! Mark, you will make me late for school.

Mark gets out, and Mary rushes past him into the bathroom.

Mom: Mary, hurry up, the bus is almost here. You will be late for school.

Mary: Mom, it's not fair, it's Mark's **fault**[3]. He took so long in the bathroom!

Mark: I told you that you should get up earlier.

Mom: Mary, I think your brother is right. You should probably get up earlier.

Mary: I have a better idea. Why don't we build a second bathroom?

Mark: Hey, that's a great idea!

Mom: **In your dreams**[4]!

[1] **battle** [batel]: *batalla*

[2] **brushing my teeth** [brashing mai tith]: *cepillarme los dientes*

[3] **fault** [falt]: *culpa*

[4] **In your dreams** [in iur drims]: *en tus sueños (ni lo pienses)*

A **Scary**[1] Night

   Mark's five-year-old brother Bobby had just gotten into bed. His mom and dad say good night. He has a night light in his room because he doesn't like the dark too much. He says he is not afraid, but he just likes it better when the night light is on. All of a sudden, he hears a noise! A **thump**[2]! His eyes are now open wide and he hears the scary sound again: thump, thump! Oh-oh, that is not good. He thinks the sound is coming from under his bed. When he hears the noise again, he calls his mom and dad. He is not crying, but his heart **is pounding**[3]. His parents come to his room and look under his bed, but find nothing. But then they all hear the mysterious noise…in the closet! Mark's father slowly opens the closet door and out races Tommy, the family cat. Mark's mother and father are so surprised that they both jump a bit. Meanwhile, Mark, who was smiling at his little **prank**[4], begins to frown when his parents look at him and realize who put Tommy in the closet. Now Mark is the one who is scared.

[1] **scary** [skeri]: *que da miedo*

[2] **thump** [thamp]: *trastazo, ruido fuerte*

[3] **is pounding** [is paunding]: *palpita fuertemente*

[4] **prank** [prank]: *travesura*

Index/Índice

¿Hay alguna palabra que quiere saber en inglés? Este índice presenta todas las palabras claves que se encuentran en este libro (salvo las de las páginas 28-30) tanto como otras palabras prácticas e interesantes seleccionadas de las frases y los pensamientos de Duke.

H I J

hambre – **hunger** 4
hora – **time** 7, 11
hueso – **bone** 6
huevos – **eggs** 4, 7
inodoro – **toilet** 21
jabón – **soap** 21
jabón líquido – **soap (liquid)** 13
jamón – **ham** 13, 14
jugar – **(to) play** 18, 19, 22, 23
jugo de naranja – **orange juice** 5, 7
jugoso – **juicy** 18

L M

lápiz – **pencil** 9, 10
lavamanos – **sink** 20, 22
lavar – **(to) wash** 22
leche – **milk** 4, 6
libreta – **notebook** 11
libro – **book** 6, 25, 26
limonada – **lemonade** 16, 19
limpiar – **(to) clean** 6
llover – **(to) rain** 15
lodo – **mud** 16, 19
maestra – **teacher** 8, 10, 11
maletín – **briefcase** 5
Mamá – **Mom** 5, 6, 7, 12, 15, 18, 22
mañana – **tomorrow** 27
mano – **hand** 22
manta – **blanket** 25
mantequilla – **butter** 4, 6
manzana – **apple** 16, 18
mermelada – **jam** 5, 6
mesa – **table** 9
mirar – **(to) look** 10, 11
mochila – **backpack** 9
mojada – **wet** 22
muñeca – **doll** 25

N O

nevera – **refrigerator** 4
niños/niñas – **children** 12, 16, 17, 20, 24
noche – **night** 24, 26
número – **number** 8
oferta especial – **special offer** 13, 14
oler – **(to) smell** 27
olvidar – **(to) forget** 14
osito – **teddy bear** 25, 26

P Q R

paleta – **lollipop** 12, 14
pan – **bread** 6, 16, 18
Papá – **Dad** 5, 6, 7, 23
papas fritas – **potato chips** 16, 19
parque – **park** 16
paseo – **(a) walk** 7
pastelito – **cupcake** 12, 15
patineta – **skateboard** 16, 19
patito – **duck (toy)** 21, 23
pecera – **fish bowl** 9, 10
pelo – **hair** 27
pelota – **ball** 17
periódico – **newspaper** 12
perro – **dog** 7, 14, 19, 22, 23
pez – **fish** 10, 11
pie – **foot** 27
pijama – **pajamas** 24
pistola de agua – **squirt gun** 21, 23
plátano – **banana** 12
plato – **dish** 4
precio – **price** 12,
puerta – **door** 9, 11
quemar – **(to) burn** 6
queso – **cheese** 12, 15, 18
radio – **radio** 21, 22

ratón – **mouse** 8, 14
regla – **ruler** 8, 10
reloj – **clock** 9, 11
resbaladilla – **slide** 16
revista – **magazine** 12, 14
robar – **(to) steal** 14
rojo – **red** 10
rueda – **wheel** 14

S T V

saber – **(to) taste** 6
sándwich – **sandwich** 15
secar – **(to) dry** 23
silla – **chair** 5, 6
subibaja – **seesaw** 16, 19
suelo – **floor** 6
supermercado – **supermarket** 12, 14
taza – **cup** 5, 7
tazón – **bowl** 4
teclado – **keyboard** 8, 10
toalla – **towel** 20, 23
tomate – **tomato** 12, 15
trabajo – **work** 7
vaso – **glass** 25, 26
ventana – **window** 9, 10

Z

zanahoria – **carrot** 12
zapatillas – **slippers** 25, 27
zapatos deportivos – **sneakers** 24, 26